GREAT OPERATIC DISASTERS

GREAT OPERATIC
DISASTERS

HUGH VICKERS

Illustrated by Michael ffolkes
With an Introduction by Peter Ustinov

Text © 1979 Hugh Vickers
Illustrations © 1979 Michael ffolkes
Introduction © 1979 Peter Ustinov

ISBN 0 333 26981 0

First published 1979 by
MACMILLAN LONDON LIMITED
*4 Little Essex Street London WC2R 3LF and Basingstoke
Associated Companies in Delhi, Dublin,
Hong Kong, Johannesburg, Lagos, Melbourne,
New York, Singapore and Tokyo*

Reprinted before publication, 1979

Printed in Great Britain by
BUTLER & TANNER LTD
Frome and London

Fourteen lines from Montague Haltrecht's *The Quiet Showman* are quoted by permission of the author and Collins ·
Publishers.

CONTENTS

To the memory of the late Aldo Piccinato – great producer and dear friend

INTRODUCTION

There is no art form which attempts the sublime while defying the ridiculous with quite the foolhardiness of opera. Even without invoking disaster, there are perils when all is going well. We often have to accept, and do so willingly, that a lady lavishly endowed with substance is an object of unrequited masculine desire simply because she is equally endowed with a voice. Things are hardly helped when her paramour is revealed to be under five foot, even with built-up shoes which make his every step across a raked stage a hazard. Matters are further complicated in this day and age by the fact that most permanent operatic troupes contain four main elements with many variations and nuances in between: those who can sing but can't act, which is perhaps the classical operatic case; those who can act but who can no longer sing, and who are often tremendously effective in smaller character roles; those paragons who can both sing and act, frequently young Americans with nowhere to go but Europe; and those who can neither act nor sing, retained in harness by some humanitarian pension scheme.

The paradoxes were surely easier to accept when the operatic stage was dominated by the first two categories, but today when suddenly confronted by thin, desirable Marguerites or Toscas, or enervating voluptuous Salomes, and tall, thin Cavaradossis, Fausts and John the Baptists, the quadruple standards are pushed further apart than ever.

The consequence of all this has been the natural one of placing critics and *cognoscenti* in orbit in a stratosphere of refinement where the true and the absurd are often indistinguishable from one another. After all, the stupidity of a stupid man is exercised in a restricted field; the stupidity of an intelligent man has a much wider diffusion, and a far greater effect, aided as it is by the element of surprise.

Experts on wine and balletomanes, bullfighting *aficionados*

7

and opera buffs have all honed their sensibilities and garlanded their vocabularies to give expression to the new subtleties of appreciation, the endless reading between invisible lines, the endless attribution of surmised intentions, the pharisaical basking in pleasures reserved for only the most exclusive ears, eyes and mouths.

Occasionally the arbiters of elegance fall out among themselves, adding to our amusement. Only the other day a distinguished critic in a great English newspaper, who shall remain nameless for the simple reason that it is not the function of those who know they are not critics to insult those who think they are by throwing their own words back at them, accorded *Nabucco* at the Paris Opéra a drubbing. This pundit accused the public of cheering its head off for half an hour (this compared unfavourably with the Swedish critic who once went out of his way to praise a performance, but had cause to end his article with the terse words 'the public failed'). In his annoyance at being outvoted, this *Feinschmecker* alleged that, despite the reign of Rolf Liebermann, the Paris public appears as provincial as it was twenty-five years ago to the outsider used to the Met. and Covent Garden, 'The difference is that it now deludes itself into believing that its taste is the height of musical sophistication.' O divine conceit! The habitués of the Met. and Covent Garden naturally believe nothing of the sort about themselves. They are above, below or beside that sort of consideration, although perhaps to a really sophisticated and knowledgeable public, like that of Osnabruck or Marseilles, Parma or Ljubljana, the nadir of provincialism may well be achieved not only in Paris, but also in New York and London.

Those who write about opera, or discuss it on radio, provide us with the smiles, the simpers and the chuckles. Now along comes Hugh Vickers with the belly-laughs, without which no consideration of the glories of opera and its attendant '*précieuses ridicules*' would be complete.

Even a superbly run establishment like the Hamburg Opera

8

is never disaster-proof. One extra fell ill before a performance of *Gotterdammerung*, but it seemed hardly worth calling a rehearsal for his replacement. After all, the only action for Schultz was to go out with Schmidt, who had done it many times before, and they would pick up the bier with Siegfried lying on it, and carry it solemnly into the wings. All the stage manager insisted upon was that Schultz look solemn. Schmidt explained the action in cursory fashion to his colleague and both men went into the canteen to while away the time. When the moment came, Schultz and Schmidt, looking solemn as hell, marched on to the stage. Each picking up one end of the bier, they found themselves facing one another. Dropping the bier, both turned outwards and lifted the bier again. Not all Wagner's genius, not all Schultz's solemnity, could prevent the stolid Hamburgers from producing a gale of laughter followed by a storm of applause. The great power and beauty of opera at its best would be lacking a dimension without a possibility of disaster, a hint of bathos. It is on a razor's edge that the finest things are invariably accomplished and it is, therefore, not an impertinence to record its disasters, but a necessary adjunct to every act of reverence.

On page 40 you will find an account of how I introduced my young daughter to opera, and with what results. I will now happily encourage her further by sending her a copy of Hugh Vickers's delightful book.

PETER USTINOV

PREFACE

HERE is a little catalogue of opera disasters – a back-handed tribute to the 'extravagant and irrational art'. They are not, I hasten to add, artistic disasters, but purely technical – caused by a bewildering variety of factors, including stage-management misfortunes, wild computers, the presence of animals on stage, the bizarre behaviour of the audience, unexpected incursions from the outside world and, by no means least, the *genius loci* of wherever the opera house is situated. All honour to the artists who ensure that these *contretemps* happen so rarely, and when they do, triumph over them with such grace....

May I gratefully acknowledge the help of many friends, especially Jim Reeve, Patric Schmid, George Shirley and Nicholas Ward-Jackson.

May 1979   HUGH VICKERS

Publishers' note

Some of the events in this book are well documented and incontrovertibly true; others have a basis in truth but have been somewhat embellished along the way; still others are almost certainly apocryphal, but '*se non è vero, è ben trovato*'. All are celebrations of the greatest of art forms, where disasters and triumphs alike are on a heroic scale.

TECHNICAL HITCHES
AND
PRACTICAL JOKES

Let us begin with the most famous of all disasters. Though it has a certain legendary quality it did really happen – and in fact I have run it to earth.

Tosca
Giacomo Puccini,
City Center,
New York, 1960

Whereas most such disasters depend on some element of misunderstanding and incompetence among the stage-management, this catastrophe is – delightfully – due entirely to ill-will, in this case between the stage staff and the soprano. With diabolical cunning they permitted her, after several stormy rehearsals, to complete her first performance without mishap until the very last moment, when Tosca throws herself off the battlements of the Castel Sant'Angelo. What normally happens is that on her cry '*Scarpia, davanti a Dio*' she hurls herself off and lands on a mattress four feet below (who but Callas has ever looked totally convincing at that moment? – Her outstretched hands haunt the memory). But in this case it was not Callas but a large young American who landed not on a mattress, but – perish the thought – on a *trampoline*. It is said that she came up fifteen times before the curtain fell – sometimes upside down, then the right way up – now laughing in delirious glee, now screaming with rage. . . . Worse still, it seems that the unhappy lady was unable to reappear in any other Opera Center performance throughout the entire season because the Center's faithful audience, remembering the trampoline, would have burst into laughter. She had to remove herself to San Francisco, where of course no such grotesque incident could possibly occur. . . .

Tosca
San Francisco
Opera, 1961

One must remember that *Tosca* is very often the Cinderella – the last opera of the season – in a big opera house. This is because it is thought to be an 'easy' opera; there are in effect only three principals – Tosca, Cavaradossi and Scarpia. Looked at from the point of view of an over-worked producer under great pressure, ninety per cent of the battle obviously lies in the principals knowing the work – the other participants amount only to the first-act chorus (some rehearsal needed here), the second-act choir (off-stage thank God) and the third-act execution squad (no problem, they don't sing . . .). Alas, it is thus that fatal errors, hideous disasters, are engendered. On this particular occasion that innocuous firing squad was composed of hurriedly enlisted and highly enthusiastic college boys from the local campus, totally ignorant of the story and constantly worrying the producer with their 'When do we come on? What do we do?' His answer was an invariable, 'Wait, wait – I'm working with the principals'. In the end, a combination of illness and a desperately tight scheddule led to the cancellation of the dress rehearsal and the appearance on the opening night of the execution squad itself only five minutes after their first and only consultation with the producer. He was still in a hurry, but felt he had given them enough to go on – 'O.K., boys. When the stage-manager cues you, slow-march in, wait until the officer lowers his sword, then shoot'. 'But how do we get off?' 'Oh – well, exit with the principals'. (This is the standard American instruction for minor characters, servants etc.)

The audience, therefore, saw the following: a group of soldiers marched on to the stage but stopped dead in its tracks at the sight of *two* people, not one as they had assumed – a man and a woman, both looking extremely alarmed. When they pointed their hesitant rifles at the man, he at first drew himself up, looking noble and resigned, but then started giving inexplicable conspiratorial sidelong glances at the women ... they pointed them at her, but she made a series of violently negative gestures – but then what else would she do if she was about to be shot? Should they, perhaps, shoot them both? But then they would hardly be standing so far apart – anyway, the opera was called *Tosca*, it was evidently tragic, the enormous woman on stage was presumably Tosca herself, solemn funereal music was playing, the officer was raising his sword. . . .

Thus it happened. By a perfectly sensible process of logical deduction they *shot Tosca instead of Cavaradossi*. To their amazement they then saw the man, some twenty yards away, fall lifeless to the ground, while the person they *had* shot rushed over to him crying (we must remember this was in a vivid American translation), 'Come on, baby, get up, we gotta go'. What could they do? They had shot one of the principals – though admittedly the wrong one – and their next instruction was '*Exit with the principals*'. In disbelief they watched as, first, Spoletta and his minions burst on to the stage and Tosca – could it be true? took up her position on top of the battlements. She jumped, and there was only one thing for it – as the curtain slowly descended the whole firing-squad threw themselves after her. . . .

Don Giovanni
W. A. Mozart,
Vienna State
Opera, 1958

Many operas end like *Tosca* with the sudden descent of the hero to some nether realm. Don Giovanni, however (as in Zeffirelli's production for Covent Garden), tends simply to disappear amid whirling clouds of stage-smoke as the chorus of off-stage demons promise him worse torments below. In Vienna, however, Cesare Siepi ended his admirable interpretation standing on a stagelift which, as so often happens, stuck halfway down, leaving his head and shoulders visible to the audience but not the rest of him. The technicians' efforts merely revealed the operation of one of the great laws governing opera disasters – that the most that can be hoped for is to restore the *status quo ante* – that is, they merely brought him back up again. Siepi then amazed the public by refusing simply to walk off and with courageous professionalism challenged the lift-operator to a second attempt. Of course exactly the same thing happened, and amid the shocked silence of the Staatsoper a single voice rang out – it is said in Italian – 'Oh my God, how wonderful – hell is full.'

Don Giovanni
City Center,
New York, 1958

Here the audience had the extraordinary experience of seeing straight through the opera to the outside world. In one of those epic accidents which haunt the dreams of stage-managers by night, *all* the scenery involved in the scene-change before Don Giovanni's feast was simultaneously raised above the proscenium level at a moment when the curtains were open and the vast doors at the back of the stage were open to admit the entry of the new set. For ten heavenly seconds, therefore, the audience saw not eighteenth-century Spain but East 55th Street – cars passing, taxis hooting, a couple of astonished traffic cops staring at them, presumably no less amazed than they – an extreme clash between reality and illusion utterly befitting New York. Indeed every city perhaps gets the disasters it deserves.

Don Giovanni
City Center,
New York, 1960

Boats, swans, balloons, horseback – even skis: opera offers so many different ways of getting on stage, each usually more accident-prone than the last. But *nothing* is more fatal than a sedan chair. On this occasion the producer decided to give one to Donna Elvira – a grandiose entrance involving two porters carrying her up a ramp behind the scene so that she could appear from the back of the steeply raked stage; she would then step out of the chair to begin '*Ah! chi mi dice mai*'.

Unfortunately she weighed a great deal and the porters only just made it up the ramp. As they arrived at the top, the one in front momentarily put his burden down, thus throwing all the weight on to the one behind – he in turn threw the chair forward, and the see-saw movement caused the soprano to turn a somersault and get stuck upside down. To make it worse, the bearers had no idea of this – indeed the very point of a sedan chair is that the porters cannot see the goings-on inside it. Unaware that anything untoward had happened, they shouldered their burden and came on to the stage unable to understand the howls of joyous laughter that greeted them. I was not there myself, but Jim Reeve, who was one of the porters, swears that she did in fact sing the whole of '*Ah! chi mi dice mai*' upside down, though he didn't himself at first realise her predicament. There was nothing for it but to let her complete the aria and then carry her off, but even then it proved impossible to extricate her from the sedan chair in the wings – she had become *identified* with it. A distraught stage-manager summoned the house firemen to smash it with their axes, and her first gesture (a fine display of traditional soprano temperament) was to

18

slap the two completely innocent bearers across the
face as hard as she could. . . .

Rigoletto
Giuseppe Verdi,
L'Opéra,
Paris, 1954

Of all the things that can go wrong with *Rigoletto* this is surely the worst, affecting what we might loosely describe as the emotional heart of the entire opera. At the very moment when the courtiers are brutally mocking him in Act II, Rigoletto's hump slid slowly down his back. As their taunts increased, the audience was puzzled to see a hunchback transformed before their eyes into a perfectly normal man – except for an enormous behind. Guy Parsons of Geneva, who witnessed this, assures me however that much more entrancing were the baritone's efforts to push the hump back up again, while singing the great cavatina beginning '*la la, la la*'. *Cortigiani, vil razza dannata*, indeed. As he points out, one would have thought they *knew* something about handling hunchbacks in Paris. . . .

Don Giovanni
King's Theatre,
Edinburgh,
1949

Fortunately it is not usually obvious to opera spectators at the Edinburgh Festival that the theatre in which they are sitting is itself a technical disaster. Naturally it is the Italian technicians who find the most difficulty – I remember the entire technical staff of the San Carlo Theatre of Naples walking out in despair after trying to set up the lighting for Cilea's *Adriana Lecouvreur* all night, only to find that on a dry Edinburgh Sunday there wasn't even a drink to be had. But even though the back stage has been greatly improved, the shallow orchestra pit continues to present an insoluble problem of balance between singers and orchestra.

The *Don Giovanni* was the Glyndebourne version but conducted by Rafael Kubelik, who became obsessed with the relationship between the Commendatore on his pedestal in the churchyard and the three trombones which accompany his pronouncements. After spending the morning trying various vantage points behind the stage the bass, David Franklin, who was hungry for lunch, facetiously suggested that he sing it from the Gents' lavatory in the passage to the greenroom. This worked so well that Kubelik, with Carl Ebert, Jani Strasser and other members of the Glyndebourne staff, insisted on the trombones playing in there with him; despite the cramped conditions out came exactly the echoing other-worldly sound required. But, alas – on the first night the unprecedented occurred – a mechanical system in the King's Theatre actually carried out its allotted task. The long-defunct automatic flush system suddenly came torrentially to life at the exact moment of '*Di rider finirai pria dell'aurora*' – and since the performance was being broadcast, B.B.C. Third Programme listeners were deluged even more powerfully than the spectators.

Talking of the Commendatore, it seems that dressing for the part can be a far from pleasant experience. Encased in canvas robes stiffened with size to suggest the marble, one still has to undergo the ordeal of the white make-up. Franklin relates how at Glyndebourne in 1938 one of the designer's assistants started flicking blobs of yellow paint at his face. 'What's that for?' he asked as one stuck in his eye. 'Well, you're a statue, aren't you?' 'So?' 'Pigeons!'

Covent Garden seasons after the war seem to have produced a number of lively incidents. The orchestra's constant teasing of the somewhat over-Germanic conductor Karl Rankl reached its climax in their launching into the overture to *Carmen* at the start of the dress rehearsal of *The Magic Flute* – 'You see, it's April Fool's Day,' explained the leader – 'It was a joke....' 'A *joke?*' Then again, we have the incident of the scene-shifters in *Die Walküre* refusing to shift the rocks – it said 'rocks' in their contract, but 'Them's not ordinary rocks, them's *Wagnerian* rocks.' Prophetic words which, one might say, launch a major *leitmotif* in post-war opera production. As for *Rigoletto* – our story concerns that admirable English tenor Walter Midgely. During '*Questa o quella*' he got the end of his moustache caught in his mouth and gradually, inexorably, sucked it in. When he finished the aria the whole thing was stuck somewhere in his windpipe, but he managed to blow it out right across the orchestra pit – by some accounts hitting Erich Kleiber in the face.

Tosca
San Diego,
1956

This is a perfect American disaster, in that in the U.S.A. they should surely depend on the unexpected malfunctioning of supposedly infallible mechanical equipment – computerise it and it *can't* go wrong. None the less one should (as we have seen) be very careful with *Tosca* – by far the most jinxed of operas, as *Macbeth* is in the theatre. In fact, I always feel great trepidation when Tosca stabs Scarpia – blood – real blood – has been drawn on at least three known occasions, once in a 1919 Rome production under Toscanini. Passions on stage have by then run so high that it seems rather modest of Tosca merely to skewer the villainous police chief with a fruit knife; one sits back relieved to think that now all she has to do is to place the candles beside the body and blow out the candelabra on the table. There are only four candles and with modern fireproofing the fire-risk is usually considered small enough to permit the use of the real thing. At San Diego, however, they were not merely electric, but the order of their going out was fixed on a computer tape along with all the rest of the lighting cues – the tape obeyed the stage-manager's signal and snuffed the candles exactly as she blew them out – except that on this occasion the programming was wrong and it blew them out in a different order from hers. She blew to the right, the candle to the left went out, she blew the back one, the one in front went out – and as she began '*E avanti a lui tremava tutta Roma*' the electronic bleep for the curtain arrived too soon and the curtain shut with furious speed before she'd finished, only to open again for the pre-set curtain-call, shutting for good at the exact moment that she and Scarpia walked forward for their applause.

A Village Romeo and Juliet
Frederick Delius,
London, 1920

This is the beautiful Delius score, conducted on that occasion by Sir Thomas Beecham with Eugène Goossens as his somewhat inexperienced assistant. If, dear reader, your knowledge of this work is confined to its charming intermezzo, 'The Walk to the Paradise Garden', let me inform you that its last act involves descent mechanisms quite comparable to those in *Tosca* and *Don Giovanni* – in fact the lovers scuttle their boat in the middle of a lake at the end of the love duet. On this occasion, Goossens, cueing the stage-management, gave the signal four pages too early and the boat sank into the lake with the lovers delivering most of the duet from under water. ... 'Very well,' snarled Sir Thomas, 'next time you can conduct it yourself.' Goossens did so, but on this occasion the cue was given four pages too late and no one was drowned at all. 'Humph – more drama in your version, I suppose.'

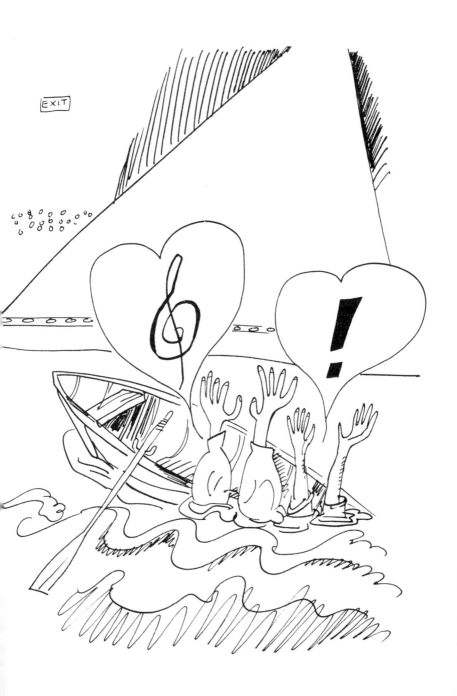

Carmen
Georges Bizet,
Mexico City,
date unknown

This performance of *Carmen* in modern dress took place in the bull-ring itself. It was a hot, heavy night in Mexico City, thirsty work for any tenor, and in the interval between Acts 3 and 4 Don José, who was an imported Italian, dashed out into the neighbouring streets to buy himself a well-earned beer. The tiny *calles* near the bull-ring are the haunts of thieves and murderers, and he hadn't gone ten yards before he was arrested by a healthy posse of policemen and dragged off to the local station. His cries were unavailing – the officers could clearly see that the man they were arresting was a disreputable soldier, probably a deserter. When he explained in mangled Spanish that he was not a deserter but an Italian tenor singing the part of a deserter, they informed him that he was drunk. He only got out by singing 'cette fleur que tu m'avais jetée' to his captors all over again.

ANIMALS

The use of horses on the operatic stage certainly goes back to the seventeenth-century Florentine masque; but I sometimes wonder if the often alarming use of animals in general may not take us back even further, to the gladiatorial contests in the Colosseum. Significantly, in 1969 a private impresario came very near to being allowed to mount a series of bullfights in the Roman Arena at Verona, between opera productions, but was prevented by the application of an obscure Fascist law originally designed for the protection of domestic pets. Unfortunately, few operas deal with persecuted Christians, though we have a fine exception in Gaetano Donizetti's *Poliuto*.

Poliuto
Rome Opera,
1951

The climactic scene in *Poliuto* occurs when the tenor renounces his love in favour of the Christian faith. The last aria is actually sung in the arena, and the producer (Aldo Piccinato) 'yielded to pressure' (his words) and agreed to present two live lions on stage, in cages, one on each side. The reaction of the big cat family to the human voice singing above the stave had not been calculated, nor were the bars of the cages close enough together. Strangely enough the animals didn't seem to mind the soprano, but when the tenor Carlo Bini reached his top C sharp, he suddenly found his shoulder gripped by an enormous paw....

One of the principles which guide Italian opera producers who decide to use animals to enhance the spectacle is that to justify the expense they must appear as often as possible. Thus the laborious procession of elephants and camels in *Aida* must appear not once, but over and over again – they constitute, as it were, a dramatic statement in themselves, like the animals in *The Magic Flute*. It all takes so long – the amount of *time* occupied in *Norma* by Pollione appearing in his chariot pulled by four horses can be immense (an attempt to vary this by using four zebras in the Baths of Caracalla, Rome, in 1938 was apparently not successful). One would hardly have thought, though, that *Carmen* could be even a possible candidate for such treatment. Not at all –

Carmen
Verona Arena,
1970

It was horses all the way – thirty-eight horses to be exact. They crossed and recrossed the stage in the background during the first act. They turned up to take José away from the inn in the second act. The third act opened with them all standing – a rather forlorn little group – on an artificial mountain. In Act IV they reappeared for Escamillo's procession, covered in Spanish finery and ridden by the picadors, but all looking alarmingly tired and nervous. In fact all went well until the very last horse made its way from the back round in a great circle to the Plaza de Toros on the right of the stage. As it approached the orchestra pit the conductor (Gianandrea Gavazzeni) gave a violent up-beat, and the horse took off towards him as if the orchestra pit was Becher's Brook. But that splendid old maestro must have worked some instant magic – the horse merely landed on the kettledrums with an enormous crash, miraculously in-

32

juring neither itself nor its rider. We waited with bated breath to see what *could* happen next – in fact it proved to be the spectacle of Gavazzeni laying down his baton (the unthinkable!) and – fatally – murmuring (forgetting that in that unique auditorium the slightest whisper is at once audible to 15,000 people) the words '*Quel piccolo finocchio di regista*' (an Italian insult better not translated).

Amid cascades of laughter the whole procession had to unwind backwards and then re-enter, this time without mishap. Judge of our amazement then, when in the last act, just as Franco Corelli was preparing to kill Grace Bumbry, a cat came bounding down from the back of the Arena (cats at Verona play much the same role as bats at Glyndebourne). Naturally attracted to whichever of the two was singing, it rubbed itself against Corelli's legs, purring and looking wistfully up as he cried 'Eh bien, damnée'.

Of course, horses out of doors in Verona, Rome or Avignon look realistic at least, but what of a single horse on stage in a theatre? Cocteau says that a real horse on stage looks like a strange mythological beast, that to make a believable theatrical horse you would have to make a completely symbolic animal of wood and canvas. The last horse I saw on stage indoors was in *Boris Godunov*.

Boris Godunov
Modest
Mussorgsky,
Royal Opera
House,
Covent Garden,
London, 1958

The libretto specifies that the Pretender – Dmitri – should appear on horseback at the head of his army. On this occasion Covent Garden had obviously grasped the point that a very large Yugoslav tenor requires a very large horse; indeed I have never seen so vast an animal outside the Yorkshire hunting field. Of course no one paid any attention to the excellently sung 'Revolution' aria, so gripped were we by what the horse might or might not do – but fortunately it was as good as gold until the applause at the end of the aria, when the horse joined in by expressing itself in the only manner obviously available to it, and in very large measure. The extraordinary thing was that when Dmitri and his followers had gone off, those erratic Covent Garden follow spotlights ('Gundogs in a snipe-infested marsh' Visconti once called them) all focused on what the horse had left, while the solitary Idiot, sitting beside it, sang of the ruin of Russia.... Indeed, no disaster, but a masterstroke of neo-Bayreuth symbolism!

Giulietta &
Romeo Riccardo
Zandonai,
La Scala,
Milan, 1913

When are we going to see this work again? It's much more exciting than Gounod's, the Bellini is too rarely given, the Berlioz is hardly an opera. In Zandonai's version Romeo gallops into exile from Verona in a snowstorm, making use of the early revolve stage, which permits a horse to gallop flat out against the stage moving at the same speed in the opposite direction. On 13 December 1913 the Scala revolve stopped in the middle of the scene and then started going forward, first unseating Romeo and then propelling his horse into the wings with the force of a rocket. Romeo was left sitting on the frantically revolving stage, a whirling, disconsolate figure, as the artificial snow kept falling.

Bernard Levin contributes this shaggy-dog story:

Carmen
Bournemouth
Date unknown

It was a Sadler's Wells tour, and they were at Bournemouth with *Carmen*. In the middle of the smugglers' scene a gigantic Pyrenean mountain dog wandered on to the stage. (Apparently, the Bournemouth theatre they were using was part of a building with offices and other rooms, and the dog, which belonged to one of the officials working there, was a very friendly beast and had the run of the building.) Many of the audience who were unfamiliar with the opera thought it was part of the scene and were delighted. (Others who knew better were doubtless even more delighted.) The dog eventually roamed down-stage opposite the conductor where it became hypnotised by the baton, which by then was being used partly to conduct the music and partly to try to shoo the beast away. Unfortunately, the dog was also used to having people throw sticks for it to fetch, and was convinced that the baton was about to be thrown. When it wasn't, the dog became cross and emitted a series of mournful barks. These, when added to by the cries of 'piss off!' which the Carmen (who had been endeavouring to kick it surreptitiously to no avail) was adding to the uproar, finally persuaded those in charge to bring the curtain down. And not a moment too soon, I imagine, except for collectors of such disasters like us who could willingly have gone on for hours longer.

As a father taking his very well-brought-up young daughter to the opera for the first time, Peter Ustinov was unwise enough to choose the Baths of Caracalla in Rome. So far we have allowed the Arena at Verona to have pride of place as far as animals are concerned, and my own memories of Caracalla are virtually limited (perforce) to the constant cries of 'Gelati, gelati!' (Ice-cream) which obliterated the entire performance – which, incidentally, was also completely invisible from where I was. Mr Ustinov must have had a better seat, because he could actually *see* that the whole stage (this was *Aida*) became at a certain point completely *covered* with animals – camels, elephants, horses, unwanted cats, etc. At a climactic point, *all* the animals relieved themselves simultaneously. As he stared aghast at this incredible sight, he felt a light tapping on his shoulder, and his daughter's earnest voice – 'Daddy, is it all right if I laugh?'

THE AUDIENCE

Some opera disasters are caused by the audience. This seems hard to believe in Anglo-Saxon countries, where the audience tends to be an essentially passive, timid body, watching the goings-on on stage with a blissfully willing suspension of disbelief. Not so in Italy, however, even today – performances often take on the character of a dialogue between audience and performers. '*Dormi, maestro*,' they cry when the music goes too slowly; '*Vai a casa!*' (Go home), I heard the Romans shout at an unfortunate tenor in *Pagliacci*, his crime being mere physical inability to repeat '*Vesti la giubba*' for a *fourth* time – poor man, he really was Pagliaccio by then – '*la gente paga è rider vuole qua. . . .*' In Parma tenors are regularly hounded to the station by dissatisfied connoisseurs, the fee they have paid to the local 'claque' humiliatingly returned to its leader, who then leads the booing. . . .

A charming audience interjection comes from –

Don Carlo
Giuseppe Verdi,
La Scala,
Milan, 1970

A very fine performance with Placido Domingo, Nicolai Ghiaurov, Martti Talvela, Shirley Verrett and Rita Orlandi Malaspina. As Claudio Abbado began the opening of King Philip's aria – an incomparable portrayal by Ghiaurov – a voice from the gods cried '*Io trovo questa musica molto lenta e noiosa*' ('I find this music remarkably slow and boring') – this *à propos* that divine cello theme, never better played. Incredible! The comment was addressed not to us, nor even to Claudio Abbado or the orchestra, but to Giuseppe Verdi, dead for over sixty years.

Certainly the audience can be insulting and annoying, but can it become physically dangerous? Yes indeed! Not for nothing did the Austrians wait for Verdi performances in Venice with fear and trepidation – in those cries of '*Viva VERDI*' was hidden the King's name – Vittorio Emanuele, Re d'Italia; every time *Nabucco* was given the theatre had to be surrounded with troops because of the audience reaction to '*Va pensiero*', that moving plaint of an enslaved people. Even in the twentieth century *Don Carlo* is still dynamite in Spain – banned from the Madrid stage throughout the Franco regime. What happens, though, if the audience identifies not merely with the general situation but with the characters themselves? For this we really have to go to Sicily....

Otello
Giuseppe Verdi,
Catania, 1963

The baritone Giancarlo Lombardi was some-what puzzled to find himself booed off stage as Iago even before he had sung the *Credo*! He made discreet enquiries, to find to his amazement that the problem lay not at all in his singing, but in the fact that his mere appearance as Iago reminded the audience too much of the traditional villain 'Gano' in the Sicilian puppet-show – Gano is the wretch who betrays the Christian knights to the Infidels. Sure enough, returning to his dressing-room the following night, he was terrified to find himself threatened by a man standing in the passage, knife in hand, hissing the word, 'Judas.' It seems Lombardi was actually lucky – according to Claudio of the Bellini Bar, Palermo, a previous exponent of the part had to dodge a hail of bullets from an infuriated marksman well positioned in the Prima Galleria.

One might well examine any possible overlap between operatic and other kinds of disasters, for example natural or political disasters. Surely this field might yield some inexplicable coincidences, some of those Jungian simultaneities.... On the political front, how strange it is that opera should be thought in the Western world to have this blandly élitist character, when revolution and sub-version of every kind forms its entire theme – was it *really* necessary for Verdi to change *Un Ballo in Maschera* from Stockholm to seventeenth-century Boston? We must remember though that the Communist world adopts the opposite approach, usually in highly exaggerated form. A splendid Handel Festival in East Berlin in 1960 described the courtly Handel as 'the people's composer – a true revolutionary' while no one who saw it could ever forget the Zagreb Opera's 1970 production of *The Magic Flute* in modern dress with the Queen of the Night as a feather-boa-ed Chicago moll in a white Rolls Royce accompanied by black gangsters ... (on second thoughts these were of course corrupt Capitalist blacks as opposed to Sarastro's good Communist negroes).

In Italy intrusions from the political world have almost but not quite caused a fiasco on many twentieth-century occasions. At the première of *Tosca* in 1900, for instance, the conductor Leopoldo Mugnone was shaking like a leaf because of a bomb threat to Queen Margherita who was present – he had good reason, since a bomb had been thrown backstage during a Toscanini *Otello* shortly before (it failed to explode) and the King – Umberto I – was in fact assassinated a few months later. Fascist violence erupted into La Scala in 1923 when Toscanini defied a group of Blackshirts who instructed him to play 'Giovinezza' before curtain-up – and again at the 1926 première of *Turandot*, unfortunately scheduled for the Fascist Empire Day – Toscanini won again with his 'Choose! It's Mussolini or me!' Today the opening of La Scala each December serves rather as a focus for leftist discontent; disaffected students, workers and others pelt the diamond-encrusted bourgeoises as they step from their limousines with '*cachi*' (persimmons) – squashy fruit about the size of an avocado pear which burst on impact into an enormous sticky yellow-red morass. This ritual act is accompanied by suitable slogans, such as '*Valpreda vi augura buon divertimento*' ('Valpreda wishes you a good time' – he is one of the left's imprisoned 'martyrs'). Next day the winter round of strikes and pay-claims can begin, and Milan grits its teeth for another '*caldo inverno*' (hot winter).

Otello
Opera/South,
New Orleans,
1955

And so to the deep South. Opera/South is an admirable institution – possibly the only all-black opera company in the world and the starting point of many of the great coloured singers now before the public. On this occasion the company embarked on *Otello*, but the illness of both the tenor and, at the last moment, his understudy obliged them to look outside the company for the lead singer. Since the only substitute available was white, the performance constituted the first known production of an all-black *Otello* with Otello as the only white man. Brilliant – of course Otello becomes in this interpretation a brutal white mercenary hired by a highly sophisticated African state – one cannot help thinking of the dramatic effect, not so much in the opera, where the librettist Boïto plays down Otello's blackness, but rather in the play, where we have but to reverse a line or two – 'Thy soul is as white as thy face ...'

WAGNERIAN EVENTS

One might have thought that the Wagner operas would yield a rich crop of unfortunate happenings, though the worst I have seen was merely a Brünnhilde at the Fenice Theatre in Venice encountering sudden visibility problems by putting on her helmet the wrong way round. In fact the old master of stage-craft seems to have made his operas very nearly disaster-proof – that is, of course, once you accept the conventions imposed by the work and whatever style of production is on offer, and of course assuming that all concerned have the sheer stamina for the task. Bernard Levin claims to have seen a *Siegfried* involving three different Siegfrieds, one for each act; the most I can offer is two Walther von Stolzings changing over between Acts II and III of *Meistersinger* (quite satisfactory if you discount the fact that one was singing in German and the other in Serbo-Croat). Very long intervals before the last third of the *Meistersinger* do, it is true, always suggest that Walther has lost his voice, which in turn inspires the delightful thought that Pogner really ought to give his daughter to the only other contestant – Beckmesser – by walkover. Not that he hasn't already won her on merit – I entirely subscribe to the admirable view of Erik Smith (of Philips) that Beckmesser's song is anyway incomparably better (especially as regards the words) than Walther's maundering rubbish. May we not hope for a modern production which will at last give us a decent ending, like the old Covent Garden Ring cycles which used to end with *Siegfried*? Some sort of justice for Beckmesser is surely not beyond the capacity of modern Wagner production; and indeed now that Patrice Chéreau has shown us that a dinner-jacketed Wotan is acceptable, one feels that a mere 'disaster'

would hardly be noticed. Perhaps the return to a 'new realism' will give us once again the chance to see at Bayreuth the (stuffed) swan shot by Parsifal fall on the head of an extra, laying him out cold. Meanwhile, here is a little gem from New York.

Lohengrin
Richard Wagner,
Metropolitan
Opera, 1936

As Lauritz Melchior – perhaps the greatest of Lohengrins – ended '*O König hör*' in the last act, the swan-boat arrived – amid that exquisite orchestral radiance – exactly on time, but alas took off again before the tenor had a chance to get into it. Trapped in what can only be called a totally untenable position, Melchior looked up at the audience and asked in the exhausted, resigned tone of one who has, say, missed the number 47 night bus '*Wenn geht der nächste Schwann?* – When does the next swan go? Apparently, he was quoting Leo Slezak, stuck thirty years before in the same position.

Perhaps apocryphally, a tenor singing the role at Covent Garden in the nineteen-fifties is said to have impaled himself particularly painfully on the swan's tail and shouted out 'Webster must go!'

Siegfried
Royal Opera
House,
Covent Garden,
London, 1937

I can't think of an opera act which rises to a single climactic moment in quite the same way as *Siegfried* Act I. One is somehow simultaneously excited on a primitive level by those barbaric cries of '*Nothung, Nothung*' and also caught up in sympathy with any tenor singing that diabolical part. (Bravo, Alberto Remedios at the English National Opera, surely emerging as the Siegfried of our generation.) As the sword is slowly forged before our eyes – symbol of the strength which will destroy Wotan's spear – we begin to wait in agonies of impatience for him to cleave the anvil on '*So schneidet Siegfrieds Schwert*'. In 1937 it was again Lauritz Melchior who squared himself to the task when – horror of horrors – the anvil fell apart three seconds before he hit it. At least that's the first occasion I know of when this occurred – according to Lionel Salter it became so regular an event that younger members of the Covent Garden audience thought it was part of the story, in the same way as they assumed that Wagner dragons would quite normally come on stage with one eye intermittently flashing and the other out. Perhaps they felt that the dragon was somehow a reflection of Wotan, with his one eye – abstruse symbolism rather than faulty wiring.

Das Rheingold
English
National Opera,
London, 1976

The first scene of the opera is set at the bottom of the Rhine, and the stage instructions call for the three Rhinemaidens to 'swim' around the stage. For this production, the whole of the stage was bathed in aqueous light and the three singers were attached to constantly rising and falling wires. It was both pretty and effective (though it must have been murder to sing in such conditions) until, one evening, very, very slowly and inexorably the safety curtain descended, at first hiding the Rhinemaidens only on their upward journeys, so that the sound of their voices was alternately muffled and *fortissimo*, and then concealing everything except occasional glimpses of their descending feet. With enormous aplomb they sang on, and it was the orchestra whose nerve failed. As the safety curtain hit the stage the music finally died away in a ragged shower of wrong notes. The management's explanation was that a leak had developed in the hydraulic system....

For the following I am again indebted to Bernard Levin –

Die Walküre
Royal Opera
House,
Covent Garden,
London, 1961

This is Hans Hotter's great fall from the mountain-top at the end of *Die Walküre*. The producer had decided to start the magic fire by having flash-bulbs explode as Wotan struck the rock with his spear, with the consequence that everybody in the house was temporarily blinded. This hardly mattered for Brünnhilde, who had after all just been put to sleep, but it caused Hotter, turning to leave the stage, to miss his footing and fall from the mountain with a crash (he was covered in stage armour) 'like a bomb hitting a corrugated-iron factory'. Presumably fearing that somebody who did not know the opera might conclude that it ends with Wotan being so struck with remorse that he commits suicide by hurling himself into the valley, Hotter gallantly climbed back into position, thus giving the audience, which had already had its money's worth and a bit over, the extra pleasure of seeing the singer's head suddenly appear from the chasm into which it had vanished, to be followed by the rest of him.

Die Walküre
Royal Opera
House,
Covent Garden,
London, 1956

Hans Hotter still remembers this slightly less alarming incident. He was for some reason delayed in putting on a new, enormous cloak before his entry in Act III – '*Wo ist Brünnhild*'. Grabbing it from the dressing-room he cast it round his shoulders and strode on to the stage, to confront an inexplicably mirthful audience. The fact was that towering above his shoulders, invisible to him, was the coat-hanger on which the cloak had been hanging. It was a fluffy, *pink* coat-hanger. He sailed through the act, his mighty stage-presence doubtless soon convincing the audience that Wotan without a coat-hanger is no Wotan at all. As Ernest Newman said, he is surely 'the only man in the world who can actually step on stage and persuade you that he is God'.

Joan Sutherland is also not an artist to be put off by minor problems of costume....

Beatrice di
Tenda
Vincenzo
Bellini,
Teatro
San Carlo,
Naples, 1961

During a performance of the last act of Luchino Visconti's magnificent staging of this unjustly neglected Bellini opera, Dame Joan's petticoat sank ever lower – and irreversibly, since Beatrice is on stage all the time. However, it was not until the final curtain-call that it hit the deck completely – to be plucked from around her feet by the tenor Renato Cioni. He waved it in the air with Latin gallantry, to the audience's cries of '*Viva, viva la Stupenda!*'

ACTS OF GOD

As we have seen, disasters are so much the stuff of opera that there seems hardly room for *real* natural disasters to obtrude on to the scene. *Al fresco* opera of course presents problems – it was alarming to see the mistral suddenly getting up during an open-air *Walküre* at the 1976 Orange Festival in the south of France and blowing all the orchestral parts away at the same moment, or the floating stage at Bregenz drifting off into the middle of the lake, complete with orchestra. Within the opera house fire is in reality the true danger, though the only major disaster of this sort for some years seems to have been the destruction of the Cairo Opera House in 1970 (with the loss of the sets and costumes for the original *Aida*) – a somewhat ironic mishap in view of the fact that the main Cairo fire-station was in fact situated in part of the opera house itself.

Flood is less common, though sets involving real water have their dangers of course –

Turandot
Giacomo Puccini,
Rome Opera,
1954

In the last scene the set showed one of those meandering oriental streams with Turandot standing on one bank and the tenor, Carlo Gasparini, standing on the other, with a little Chinese-Milanese rustic bridge between them. Gasparini's instructions were simple – when she cries '*Mio nome è Amor!*' he was to turn, charge across the bridge and grasp Turandot in his arms. In fact, he turned, charged, forgot the bridge, tried to leap the stream, tripped and fell in, thus very nearly joining the disconsolate ranks of Turandot's former admirers. . . . A real earthquake might make a very effective interjection in a great many operas, but I know of only one case –

Cavalleria Rusticana
Pietro Mascagni,
San Francisco,
1938

With Lily Pons, no less. She made her entry as Santuzza in a 'Sicilian' donkey cart – *you* know, ethnic painting all over it, and the donkey wearing a straw hat with holes for its ears. Suddenly there came that unnerving quivering which every inhabitant of San Francisco experiences from time to time. It was too much for the donkey. With a great shrieking *eeeaw* he leapt in the air and charged across the stage, throwing Lily Pons out of the back of the cart and bringing down all the scenery.

But perhaps the most dramatic of nature's interventions occurred during the first night of Frédéric d'Erlanger's opera based on Thomas Hardy's *Tess of the d'Urbervilles.* According to the Hardy scholar Dr Desmond Hawkins, d'Erlanger wrote to Hardy from Milan in April 1906, complaining that 'Mount Vesuvius behaved most unkindly to me' and that his weeks of patient rehearsal in Naples had been rewarded during the first act by a violent eruption. The audience was in any case small – as the population had feared an eruption for some days – and their 'state . . . it is hardly necessary for me to describe'. The theatre was closed down next day by the municipality, despite a 'hearty reception' and favourable press coverage for that part of the opera which the terrified company had managed to present. When Hardy heard of this *débâcle*, he remarked, characteristically, that it was only to be expected, as being all of a piece with Tess's career.

Vesuvius seems, indeed, to have a certain antipathy towards the intrusion into Naples of English opera plots – and heroines, for that matter. It had already erupted before during the San Carlo debut of Mrs Billington, the first great English soprano of the early nineteenth century. She was howled off the stage by an infuriated audience who considered that the mountain was rightly protesting against the appearance at the San Carlo of a 'Protestant heretic'. (Fortunately she was able to find some consolation in the simultaneous loss of her unwanted husband, a double-bass virtuoso she had married at sixteen.) Actually, the attitude of Neapolitans towards their opera-house *is* very emotional. I was talking to one during an interval at La Scala who insisted that the essence of the San Carlo is that it is *'maschio'* (masculine). 'What about the Fenice in Venice?' I hazarded. *'Ah, quella è femmina.'* 'And this one here?' (looking around at the glorious Scala). A sneer. *'Questo qui, caro signore, questo è neutro.'*

'HAIR-BREADTH SCAPES'

Perhaps we should end by recalling some of the innumerable occasions when disaster has been averted by inspired improvisation and a masterly understanding of the exigencies of the moment. Somehow the march of events in opera prevents memory loss, for instance, from being quite so dangerous as in the straight theatre – one can't quite imagine in an opera house the famous story about Gielgud and Richardson who, after listening to a prompt three times in complete silence, turned to the prompter with the words 'We know the line, man, we just can't remember which of us says it'. On the other hand, the act of singing as you plunge on to the stage is so nerve-wracking that an entry at the wrong moment is quite a hazard, as is a sudden, immediate freeze – I remember idiotically remarking to a soprano in the wings 'I bet you can't even remember which opera this is' – sure enough she stepped on stage and couldn't. Even Tito Gobbi's début at La Scala, as a Herald in Pizzetti's *Orseolo* (conducted by the composer), consisted in bawling out the words '*La Signoria del Doge e del Senato*' half a minute too soon, in the middle of Tancredi Pasero's most important aria. '*Cretino, chi t'ha mandato qui?*' (Idiot, who sent you here?) were therefore the first words addressed to Gobbi from the Scala rostrum. . . . Here, however, is something for connoisseurs of *averted* disaster –

The Magic Flute
Glyndebourne Festival, 1964

In Franco Enriquez and Emmanuele Luzzati's enchanting production the scenery consisted of a number of free-standing triangular pillars, on each face of which a different coloured pattern was painted. Thus, for the scene to change from, say, the forest to Sarastro's temple, the stagehand inside each pillar merely turned round through 120 degrees. Near the beginning of the second half of the opera, during a snatch of dialogue between Heinz Blankenburg as Papageno and Ragnar Ulfung as Tamino, two unfortunate stagehands lost their balance and crashed, complete with pillars, to the ground, letting out involuntary and clearly audible cries for help as they did so. Blankenburg looked at Ulfung, Ulfung looked at Blankenburg, and together they walked backstage and with much ad-libbing in German – including a free advertisement for the strength-giving powers of Guinness – heaved the pillars upright again. Rubbing their hands with satisfaction they then returned to the front of the stage to continue the opera – but not before the Glyndebourne audience, as always in a jovial mood after the dinner interval, had burst into a tremendous round of applause.

Nor are singers a whit less resourceful, as anyone who works with them knows. At a production of my own of Philidor's *Blaise le Savetier* at the French Institute, London, 1976, a quarter-inch steel pin was supposed to hold in place the false front of the *armoire* in which the philandering landlord, Monsieur Pince, is hiding. Watching in the wings, I was appalled to see the pin break and the *armoire* door begin slowly to open (thus destroying the entire plot) when, with an ease which positively enhanced the dramatic situation, the tenor Emile Belcourt as the outraged husband casually leant against it for the exact amount of time required for Garrick Jones within to get a grip on it – the audience of course noticing nothing in the excitement of the near-confrontation between husband and lover. Belcourt as Loge is of course also – like most Loges – a doughty hand at rebuilding the pile of gold which the stupid gods have knocked down (or rather, the designer and producer have made incapable of standing up) with a scornful and supercilious expression exactly fitting the character. A yet more charming example of stage improvisation, however, is this from *The Quiet Showman*, Montague Haltrecht's life of Sir David Webster:

Die Walküre
Covent Garden
Manchester,
1956

The performance was a splendid one, conducted by Reginald Goodall and with the famous Hilde Konetzni as Sieglinde. He [Sir David] loved describing the moment of great ecstasy in the love duet when quite suddenly she performed a beautiful sweeping movement, one he'd not seen before, and ended kneeling at her lover's feet. He was deeply moved, and tears sprang to his eyes. He would go on to explain that what had actually happened was that the lady had *lost a tooth* and had seen it caught in the light – gleaming like Rhinegold! Her swooping joy was the joy of discovery, not the ecstasy of love. There was panic in the interval, with Konetzni not at all sure she could continue with a tooth missing. Stage director Elizabeth Latham happily had an inspiration. Wouldn't chewing-gum keep it in? She sent out for some. It worked. it *just* kept the tooth steady for the rest of the performance.'

Siegfried
Royal Opera House,
Covent Garden,
1955

However, even worse than a Sieglinde losing her tooth is surely a Siegfried who loses his sword. At Covent Garden the property-master seemed to have grasped the idea that Siegfried has to forge a complete sword from various pieces, but not the fact that he must finally be able to show the audience the finished article and even split an anvil with it. Alas it was not until halfway through the forging scene that Wolfgang Windgassen realised that only the fragments had been supplied, and he was therefore faced with the urgent necessity of actually forging Nothung in good earnest, for the first time in the history of the *Ring*, and on an anvil made of cardboard. Responding calmly to the challenge, he allowed his run-up to the anvil to take him further and further towards the wings, where he managed to collect the complete sword and bring it on under his cloak undetected by the audience....

Don Giovanni
City Center,
New York,
1960

A terrified new Don Ottavio mentally reversed the order of his arias, walked on stage and began '*Il mio tesoro*' instead of '*Dalla sua pace*'. It is said that the orchestra, under Julius Rudel, had such mastery of the score that as one man they instantaneously cut to the correct bar a hundred odd pages later, with such aplomb that the audience assumed that for some reason the arias had been deliberately reversed....

A notable example of cool teamwork between Tito Gobbi and an unknown member of the Covent Garden chorus is recounted in the great singer's autobiography *My Life*.

Un Ballo in Maschera
Royal Opera House
Covent Garden,
1954

Gobbi was rushed in at an afternoon's notice to replace an indisposed Anckerstroem, only to find that the production was in the original version – eighteenth-century Sweden instead of seventeenth-century Boston. Gobbi had not been informed of this and had never sung in the Swedish version. His experience therefore, though doubtless extremely puzzling, did not become positively alarming until the last act, when he suddenly realised that he lacked a knife to assassinate Gustavus III – otherwise the Earl of Warwick – indeed, that his position was that of our soldiers in *Tosca* but in reverse – he knew whom to execute but not how. The chorus-member managed to read his mind and, incredibly, to obtain a pistol (presumably from one of the guards). 'What do I need a pistol for?' mutters Gobbi, still all set for the stabbing. 'You *shoot* him, now!' And Anckerstroem gave his rival the *coup de grâce* with the correct weapon.

Finally, Peter Ustinov found himself directing an opera in what is without doubt *the* most technically advanced opera stage in the world – the Hamburg Opera House. (If, as one hopes, the Covent Garden appeal is successful, its backstage facilities will equal those of modern Hamburg.) There, whole sets wait in an enormous structure beside the wings and slide into place at the touch of a button. The technicians are quite incredibly efficient, and yet – there was one man who was totally hopeless. With him, everything went wrong. He dropped a hammer from the flies, narrowly missing the Stage Director's head. Whole sets fell down as he approached. The computerised lighting track went bananas and darkness fell over all. . . . Eventually Mr Ustinov asked him to explain exactly who he was and why they kept him on. 'Ah, you see, they keep me here to *humanise* them.' An admirable reply, but surely there must be more to it than that. Ustinov went on to ask, 'But *why* do you in fact make all these incredible mistakes?' 'Ah, you see, it's a long family tradition.' 'What? You mean there are *more* of you, a whole *family*?' 'Oh yes – you should have seen my father.' 'What did he do?' 'Well, he was Stage Director of the Klagenfurt Opera and he made the most incredible mistakes, much worse than anything of mine . . . But – one day he achieved the impossible – he got it *all* right. The opera was *William Tell*, very much the thing for Klagenfurt of course, and watching from the stage manager's place in the wings, he could *see* that it was perfect – all the sets in place, the chorus in position, the animals behaving, the prompter prompting, the singers singing and the orchestra (audibly) playing.' 'So what went wrong?' 'Oh just one little thing – *the curtain never went up.* . . .'

And in those days it could have been possible. Just.

The Ultimate Disaster

INDEX

A

Abuse, from audience, 42, 43, 44, 45, 61
Acoustics, unfortunate, 33
Ad-libbing, 65
Adriana Lecouvreur (Cilea), 22
Aida (Verdi), 32, 40, 58
Al fresco opera, dangers inherent in, 58
Anckerstroem (*Un Ballo in Maschera*), 69
Anglo-Saxon audiences, passivity of, 42
Animals, aggressive, 30
   impervious to artistry, 30
   incontinent, 35, 40
   over-affectionate, 33
   recycled, 32
   unexpected behaviour of, 32–3, 39
Anvils, fragile, 51
Audiences, hostile, 42, 43, 44, 45, 61
Avignon, 34

B

Ballo in Maschera, Un (Verdi), 44, 69
Baritones, disasters involving, 16, 21, 44, 64, 69
Basses, disasters involving, 16, 22–3, 53, 54
Bats, at Glyndebourne, 33
Bayreuth, 50
B.B.C., unexpected good fortune of listeners to, 22–3
Beatrice di Tenda (Bellini), 54
Becher's Brook, orchestra pit mistaken for, 32
Beckmesser, under-rated, 48
Beecham, Sir Thomas, 26
Bellini, Vincenzo, 32, 36, 54
Bini, Carlo, 30
Bizet, Georges, 24, 28, 32, 39
Blaise le Savetier (Philidor), 66
Blankenburg, Heinz, 65
Boats, dangerous to tenors, 50
   prematurely scuttled, 26
Boïto, Arrigo, 46
Bomb, unexploded, 45
Boris Godunov (Mussorgski), 34, 35
Bournemouth, canine disaster at, 39
Bregenz, 58
Brünnhilde, temporarily blinded by helmet, 48
Bumbry, Grace, 33

Index

K

Kettle drums, landing-strip for horse, 32–3
Klagenfurt Opera, 71
Kleiber, Erich, 24
Konetzni, Hilde, 67
Kubelik, Rafael, 22

L

La Scala, Milan, 36, 43, 45, 62, 64
  indeterminate gender of, 62
Lingerie, escaped, 54
Lions, dislike of high notes, 30
Lohengrin (Wagner), 50

M

Magic Flute, The (Mozart), 24, 32, 45, 65
Mascagni, Pietro, 60
Mastersingers, The (Wagner), 48
Meistersinger, Die (Wagner), 48
Melchior, Lauritz, 50, 51
Memory, ill-timed loss of, 64
Metropolitan Opera, *see* New York
Mexican police, philistine attitude of, 28
Midgely, Walter, 24
Milan, *see* La Scala
Moustache, Duke of Mantua's, swallowed, 24
Mozart, Wolfgang Amadeus, 16, 17, 18, 22, 24, 32, 45, 65, 68
Mugnone, Leopoldo, 45
Mussolini, weighed against Toscanini and found wanting, 45
Mussorgsky, Modest, 35

N

Nabucco (Verdi), 43
Naples, *see* San Carlo
Neapolitans, an emotional people, 61–2
Newman, Ernest, 52
New Orleans, 46
New York, City Opera, 12, 17, 18, 68
  Metropolitan Opera, 50
Norma (Bellini), 32